Self Work 101

(Workbook)

A Guide to Self-Improvement
and the Journey
to Personal Freedom

Copyright © 2024 Bianca Gibson

All rights reserved. No part of this publication may be reproduced, distributed, or transmitted in any form or by any means, including photocopying, recording, or other electronic or mechanical methods, without the prior written permission of the publisher, except in the case of brief quotations embodied in critical reviews and certain other noncommercial uses permitted by copyright law. For permission requests, write to the publisher, addressed "Attention: Permissions Coordinator," at the address below.

Paperback ISBN: 978-1-63616-225-6

Published By Opportune Independent Publishing Co.
www.opportunepublishing.com

Printed in the United States of America

For permission requests, please email the publisher with the subject line as "Attention: Permissions Coordinator" to the email address below:
Info@Opportunepublishing.com

DEDICATION

First and foremost, I dedicate this SELF workbook to myself and my travels. Unknowingly, until now, maybe my readers were not aware that most of this workbook was written during my travels around the world. With over 20 years of traveling experience, I indulge in self-care, self-reflection, self-motivation, solitude and more. I'd also add that even during some struggles and troublesome times in my life, I was inspired to encourage others through my powerful life experiences as I've shared briefly throughout my first Self- work 101 workbook. My travels have inspired me in so many ways and they were the most liberating and peaceful times of my life, which makes this SELF book so inspiring and meaningful to share with others. It is my hope that you gain more understanding of your life through the innovative, educational information this book has to offer. I also wish you well on your 101-day journey to rediscover, redefine and renew your potential through intentional lessons that focuses on self-awareness, self-reflection and self-motivation and ultimately self-care as you pace yourself and implement the new and refreshing embarkment of SELF- work 101 A-Z.

— Gentle Regards,

Bianca G.

HOW TO USE SELF-WORK 101 A-Z

As a continuation of the Self-work 101 interactive workbook, Self-work 101 A-Z has been created to assist readers with guidance, exploration and preparation as you embark on your newly profound journey of clarity, peace and freedom. In Section One, you will find the following sections to be precise and thought-provoking. Jump into:

Lesson sections

Key points to ponder —starting with A and going to Z — with positive phrases that supports the subtitle in which you will explore in depth.

Subtitles: definitions and explorations of the section phrases that lead to the lesson questions.

Lesson questions: More in-depth exploration with open-ended questions that help you to identify, understand and acknowledge areas for growth and appreciation.

365 on ME Questionnaire: The closed-ended questions, with further exploration, are intentionally designed to help you think more in-depth as this expansion will identify and perhaps touch some untouched emotions in which you were not aware you'd possess.

Reflection: Utilize this space to process all information you've discovered, learned and will apply from each section you've worked on today. You will also find examples as well as demonstrations to help guide you throughout each section/lesson.

The writer urges readers to utilize this workbook as instructed, starting with the first lesson and working your way throughout the book to receive the full potential of your journey. In Section Two, you will find the following more detailed information and instructions to follow:

Self-observation: Utilize this space to provide detailed information regarding your demonstration of the previous lesson and/or experience you have encountered. For instance, if the previous lesson was self-disciplined, you will write about your ability to display self-discipline, situations, persons involved and more.

Key word(s) to ponder: Words from table of contents, used for exploration and demonstration of practicing skills.

Questions to ponder: Three realistic questions to ponder when making a decisions to move forward in life.

Hindrance and rid the waste: Deciding what it is that keeps you from becoming the very best version of who you desire to be and stamping a date of when you will decide to no longer allow that person, place or thing to hold you back from moving forward in life.

Our 101 A-Z SELF begins now!

TABLE OF CONTENTS

Self-esteem
Exploring Self-esteem
Self-love
Experience
Determination
Unique (ness)
Self-confidence
Strength
Growth
Self-care
Consistency
Experiences
Persistence
Manifestation
Motivation
Self-discipline
Growth Part 2:
Self-awareness
Choosing
Balance
Resilience
Change
Serenity
Mindfulness
Reward
Self-discipline Part 2:

Elevation
Calmness
Relaxation
Manifestation Part 2:
Self-assurance
Peace
Healing
Comfort
Dignity
Self-admiration
Beauty
Courage
Inspiration
Determination Part 2:
Perseverance
Understanding
Self-concept
Wisdom
Knowledge
Responsibility
Mindset
Accountability
Realization
Empath
Wellness
Purpose

Self-educate
Boldness
Evaluation
Self-discovery
Attitude
Self-Investment
Potential
Renew
Fierce
Insight
Energy
Ambition
Meditation
Critical Thinking
Influence
Reevaluate
Explore
Mentality
Venture
Power
Feel (ings)
Commitment
Ability
Evolution
Impact
Nurture
Preparation
Transformation
Reset
Transition

Transparency
Execution
Vision
Productivity
Pursuit
Stability
Intrigue
Envision
Diligence
Embody
Patience
Assertiveness
Tranquility
Possibility
Bravery
Receptive
Modest
Freedom

Let's get into it!

What is it that you desire to gain from this journey of SELF-WORK 101 A-Z?

_____

_____

_____

_____

The 365 on ME questionnaire is designed for you to be open and honest with yourself, for yourself. More specifically, you will find that each questionnaire answer requires elaboration. The closed-ended questions, with further exploration, are intentionally designed to help you think more in-depth as this expansion will identify and perhaps touch some untouched emotions in which you were not aware you'd possess. Be kind, be gentle, but be real with yourself while expanding this section. This portion of the book is to help you explore confusion, define uncertainty and confront any doubt that could be restricting and causing you to be uncomfortable and/or unsure of your own potential.

SECTION 1

Key points to ponder:
Assertive—having or showing a confident and forceful personality.
Ambition (ambitious)—having or showing strong desire and determination to succeed.
Affable—friendly and good-natured.

Self-esteem | ˌself-ə-ˈstēm | —confidence and satisfaction in oneself.

LESSON QUESTIONS

Describe your ability to allude to self-esteem even when faced with uncharted challenges.

_____

_____

_____

Using all key points to ponder, how are you able to demonstrate each as this shows you're confident and certain of yourself? Example: I am an assertive person when I am focused on reaching a goal. When challenged to complete a task, I am ambitious with unwavering faith. Even when faced with difficult situations, I remain affable and respectful.

_____

_____

_____

_____

_____

365 on ME Questionnaire – Elaborate on each answer to the questionnaire.

1. On a scale from 1-10 (1 being least and 10 being greatest), if you chose number 6, does this mean that you are not fully confident and secure in how you feel about yourself, overall?

    Yes _____
    No _____
    Undecided _____

2. Have you allowed the opinions of others (about you) to deter you from thinking positively and confidently about your abilities?

    Yes _____
    No _____
    Undecided _____

REFLECTION

Utilize this space to process all information you've discovered, learned and will apply from each section you've worked on today.

_____
_____
_____
_____
_____
_____
_____

SECTION 2

Key points to ponder:
Brave- courageous, valiant(heroic).
Balanced- emphasizes stability and equilibrium.
Benevolent- having a desire to do good.

EXPLORING SELF-ESTEEM

Now that we have gotten geared up and ready to further explore self-esteem, let's set focus on the person you are today versus the person you were this time last year. How have you grown? In what ways or areas have you grown? Does this growth reflect the way that you feel about yourself?

_____

_____

_____

_____

LESSON QUESTIONS

Instructions: Complete questions 1 and 2 by using the proper key points to ponder to complete each question/sentence, then answer the questions you've created. You may use key points more than once if you desire.

1. If I desire to be the very best me, what are some positive traits that describe my ability to be _____ and resilient regardless of what I am faced with?

_____

_____

_____

2. Even when times are challenging, I know that I am creating _____ in my life that will keep me disciplined, focused and _____.
   Therefore, what is it that keeps me motivated to become the best version of myself?

   _____

   _____

   _____

365 on ME Questionnaire – Elaborate on each answer to the questionnaire.

1. Are there people or situations that have caused you to feel defeated and/or that you're not operating in your best version of who you desire to be?

   Yes _____
   No _____
   Undecided _____

2. When you are alone and away from others, do you feel that you can accomplish and achieve tasks independently?

   Yes _____
   No _____
   Undecided _____

REFLECTION

Utilize this space to process all information you've discovered, learned and will apply from each section you've worked on today.

_____

_____

_____

_____

_____

_____

_____

SECTION 3

Key points to ponder:
Captivating- having the power to attract and hold attention.
Candescent- glowing or starting to glow with heart.
Candid- being honest and straightforward, expressing opinions or feelings.

Self-love | self-'ləv |—Love of self, such as an appreciation of one's own worth or virtue.

LESSON QUESTIONS

1. In your own words, what does self-love mean to you, and how do you demonstrate self-love?

    _____

    _____

    _____

2. Using each key to ponder, complete a sentence that describes self-love and how the key ponder relates to your demonstration of self-love.

    Sentence 1: _____

    Sentence 2: _____

Sentence 3: _____

365 on ME Questionnaire – Elaborate on each answer to the questionnaire.

1. To be completely raw and honest with yourself, are there times when you don't feel like you deserve self-love?

   Yes _____
   No _____
   Undecided _____

2. Are you practicing self-love in all areas of your life or only when someone mentions it and/or when you have acquired such self-help material, such as this book?

   Yes _____
   No _____
   Undecided _____

REFLECTION

Utilize this space to process all information you've discovered, learned and will apply from each section you've worked on today.

_____

_____

_____

_____

_____

_____

SECTION 4

Key points to ponder:
Dauntless- fearless and determined, showing courage and bravery in the face of adversity.
Dedicated- committed; commitment.
Determined- showing courage and bravery.

EXPLORING SELF-ESTEEM

September 1, 2015, my son and I migrated to Houston, Texas from McDonough, Georgia. No family, only a friend and her family, I unrooted and transitioned to a much larger city, taking on a job making only $12.50 from a healthy salary of over $6k a month, 2 paid off vehicles, living in my 2,200 sq ft 2-story, 4 bedrooms, and 2.5 bathrooms home in south Atlanta. Now, one would say are you insane to leave all of that and downsize tremendously! Not only did I leave my job making almost 3 times more than I was making at my first job in Texas, but my mortgage was only $650 in this beautiful spacious home and neighborhood to paying twice that amount in a small 2-bedroom apartment. HAHA, clearly, I was delusional, right? Or were I determined, dedicated, and demonstrated at dauntless spirit because I knew that my start wouldn't be my forever! TODAY, and for about 6 of the 9 years of residing in Texas, not only have I maximized a 6-figure salary, healthy investments and savings, but I became a published author and have maintained consistency in selling and presenting my books in bookstores and venues. I've also met some really amazing and influential people that have motivated me to take my skills and expertise to another level. I am also a certified life coach. The point is, your current situation whether okay, barely making it, or maintaining it, can change but only if you desire to take a risk and allow yourself to explore that courageous spirit that resides deeply inside of your soul. I DID!!

LESSON QUESTIONS

1. Write here what it is that keeps you from being able to demonstrate your ability to be dauntless in exploring and experiencing a challenge. If you cannot identify any, write ways in which you have demonstrated dauntless traits.

_____

_____

_____

_____

2. Name two to three things or people that you are dedicated to and why.

_____

_____

_____

3. What keeps you determined to get things done?

_____

_____

_____

365 on ME Questionnaire – Elaborate on each answer to the questionnaire.

1. Do you have the spirit of a winner? (*Hint*: A winner is whatever you believe it is. However, you decide if you have accomplished enough.)

    Yes _____
    No _____
    Undecided _____

2. Are you afraid to step outside of your comfort zone and allow yourself to explore and experience the unknown?

    Yes _____
    No _____
    Undecided _____

REFLECTION

Utilize this space to process all information you've discovered, learned and will apply from each section you've worked on today.

_____
_____
_____
_____
_____
_____
_____
_____
_____
_____
_____
_____
_____
_____
_____

SECTION 5

Key points to ponder:
Eager- enthusiastic, strong desire.
Ebullient- high spirits, bringing contagious joy and energy.
Endearing- inspiring affection, love or fondness.

Determination | di-tər-mə-nā-shən | —Firmness of purpose; resoluteness.

LESSON QUESTIONS

1. When you feel defeated or unmotivated to get things done, how are you able to regain the mental strength to complete task(s)?

   _____

   _____

2. Complete the sentence using each of the key points to ponder.

   I understand that there will be times when I don't feel like doing the things that I need to do. In these times, I will reset my focus and find joy in knowing that I am _____ , and I demonstrate the ability to become _____ .Even when the odds are against me, I will possess the spirit of _____ .

365 on ME Questionnaire - Elaborate on each answer to the questionnaire.

1. In times of despair and uncertainty, are you able to identify what it is that causes you to feel less eager to get things done?

   Yes _____
   No _____
   Undecided _____

2. When you are determined to complete tasks or even make up your mind to address a difficult situation, does your motivation come from your desire to gain resolution or closure?

Yes _____
No _____
Undecided _____

REFLECTION

Utilize this space to process all information you've discovered, learned and will apply from each section you've worked on today.

_____
_____
_____
_____
_____
_____
_____
_____
_____
_____
_____

SECTION 6

Fierce-ferocious, strong temperament.
Faith-filled- full of strong belief; trust in a higher power demonstrating resilience.
Factual- accuracy and truthfulness.

Uniqueness | yoo-neek-nis | —A state or condition wherein someone or something is unlike anything else in comparison, or remarkable, or unusual.

FACT CHECK POINT

No one knows what it takes to be you.

LESSON QUESTIONS

Complete the following by revising each quote while using key points to ponder.

1. I am me, and there's isn't another person like me; therefore, I know that this is factual and authentic.

   _____
   _____

2. I love being the beautiful soul that I am because not only am I different but I'm fierce and unmovable.

   _____
   _____

3. I am steadfast and firm on my own principles and values, which also builds my faith-filled spirit that also separates me from others.

   _____
   _____

365 on ME Questionnaire – Elaborate on each answer to the questionnaire.

1. Are there obstacles that prevent you from being your authentic self?

    Yes ____
    No ____
    Undecided ____

2. Does being unique or different from others cause you to feel like an outcast?

    Yes ____
    No ____
    Undecided ____

REFLECTION

Utilize this space to process all information you've discovered, learned and will apply from each section you've worked on today.

_____
_____
_____
_____
_____
_____
_____
_____
_____

SECTION 7

Key points to ponder:
Genuine- authenticity and sincerity.
Gallant- Evokes the notion of bravery, courage, and chivalry.
Grateful- warm, friendly feelings towards something.

Quick note from the author:
Chest out, chin up, set your eyes to focus on the tunnel vision that no one else can see but you. Now go, go far, go wide, go up, and side to side, but don't you dare look down. There's nothing underneath your feet that should pique your interest. All things that are afar will seemingly come close as long as you stay focused. Sure, obstacles will always come, and sometimes, we become distracted, but unwavering belief will help to reset your attention and it is then that you WILL experience a bigger and bolder YOU!

—With Immersive Intent,
Coach B

Strength | strengkth |—The capacity of an object or substance to withstand great force or pressure.

LESSON QUESTIONS

1. How has your strength been tested? During this trial, how did you demonstrate a gallant spirit to withstand amid adversity?

_____

_____

_____

_____

_____

2. When you demonstrate strength, does it reflect previous situations you've experienced that has equipped you with knowledge and power to get through it? If so, explain how you've remained your genuine authentic self during these times.

_____

_____

_____

_____

_____

_____

365 on ME Questionnaire - Elaborate on each answer to the questionnaire.

1. Are there times when you feel as if you failed to show strength due to fear and/or not feeling confident in your own ability to persevere?

    Yes ____
    No ____
    Undecided ____

2. Are you truly and genuinely grateful for some of the tough times you've experienced because they have prepared you for even tougher times?

    Yes ____
    No ____
    Undecided ____

REFLECTION

Utilize this space to process all information you've discovered, learned and will apply from each section you've worked on today.

_____
_____
_____
_____
_____
_____
_____
_____
_____
_____

SECTION 8

Key points to ponder:
Healthy - having good health; "doing well."
Happy - feelings of joy, satisfaction, contentment and fulfillment.
Hopeful - optimism about the future.

TASK – Take time to just breathe:

🕮 Look, I know that this can be a very challenging task to achieve, especially if you're a person who has a full list of responsibilities and is pressing for time management and juggling life. Things get hectic, and before you know it, things continue to pile up. I get it, I really do. However, I also know that it is imperative to take time to do absolutely nothing but relax; this contributes to overall wellness mentally, emotionally, physically and spiritually. During this time of just breathing, of course the brain continues to operate in the way we allow its capacity. This means we get to choose how much and exactly what we allow to consume our thoughts. Yes, it takes practice and perhaps constant meditation, but it can be achieved. I challenge you to reset your focus today by taking the time to pause and just breathe. My second published book, Pause on Purpose, teaches the reader to focus on the mind, body and spirit while practicing meditation as well as other relaxation techniques. Immediately after reading this section of the book, take 10 minutes to focus your attention on your breathing only —the rise and fall of your chest, the breath s that you take and your breathing labor, in through your mouth and releasing through your nose. It may be difficult to focus the very first time, but attempt this as many times as you can, until you come closer to achieving 10 minutes of just breathing. Go forth, and give yourself grace if you find it difficult to complete this task. Just don't ever stop trying!

—On Purpose,
Coach B

Growth | ˈgrōth |—The process of increasing.

LESSON QUESTIONS

1. Define your own meaning of personal growth. How have you grown in the past six months?

_____

_____

_____

2. When you're happy or expressing joy, in what ways are you able to demonstrate mental and emotional growth?

_____

_____

_____

3. Describe what it means when you are focused on your mental, spiritual, emotional and financial health.

_____

_____

_____

365 on ME Questionnaire - Elaborate on each answer to the questionnaire.

1. Are there times when you find yourself more focused on material and tangible stability and not as much on your mental and emotional well-being (for instance, you're focused on your job, designer clothes and shoes, and/or money)?

    Yes _____
    No _____
    Undecided _____

2. Do you experience moments when you are hopeful even when the odds seem to be against you?

    Yes _____
    No _____
    Undecided _____

REFLECTION

Utilize this space to process all information you've discovered, learned and will apply from each section you've worked on today.

_____
_____
_____
_____
_____
_____
_____

SECTION 9

Key points to ponder:
Intuitive- curiosity, possessing or given to intuition or insight.
Idyllic- extremely pleasant, simple and peaceful.

Self-care | ˌself-ˈker | — Care for oneself.

POSITIVE AFFIRMATIONS

Please complete each affirmation as instructed below.

Ex. I am beautiful in every way.

I am beautiful _____

I am resilient _____

I am strong _____

I am confident _____

I am enough _____

LESSON QUESTIONS

1. In what ways have you been able to use your intuitive ability to gain knowledge or motivation to attend your own self-care?

   _____

   _____

2. Even on days or times when you don't feel your best mentally and emotionally, what are some self-help tools that you can utilize to maintain or evoke an idyllic perspective?

   _____

   _____

365 on ME Questionnaire - Elaborate on each answer to the questionnaire.

1. Do you make excuses for not tending to yourself-care due to financial instability?

   Yes _____
   No _____
   Undecided _____

2. When you engage in self-care, do you focus on the fulfillment of how it makes you feel emotionally, physically and spiritually?

   Yes _____
   No _____
   Undecided _____

REFLECTION

Utilize this space to process all information you've discovered, learned and will apply from each section you've worked on today.

_____

_____

_____

_____

_____

_____

_____

_____

_____

_____

SECTION 10

Key points to ponder:
Jovial- hearty, joyous and humorous fellowship.
Jaunty- full of confidence and energy

Consistency | kən-ˈsi-stən(t)-sē | —An agreement or harmony of parts of features to one another or a whole.

FACT CHECK POINT

A tree receives water and sun to flourish. There are four stages in the tree growth process (seed, stem, sapling and full-grown tree). Like a tree, we flourish when we are consistent and receiving care, love and support . Continue to water your soil (soul) and dance in the sun (light), even when you don't feel like it. Consistency produces growth.

—Positively Aligned,
Coach B

LESSON QUESTIONS

1. In what areas (mentally, physically, emotionally, financially and spiritually) have you demonstrated consistency?

   _____

   _____

   _____

2. When you are consistently working on becoming a better you for you, in what ways do you demonstrate a jovial and jaunty spirit?

   _____

   _____

   _____

365 on ME Questionnaire - Elaborate on each answer to the questionnaire.

1. Do you allow what others think of you to interfere with your ability to be consistent in specific areas in your life?

   Yes _____
   No _____
   Undecided _____

2. Do you personally believe that being consistent in your life has helped you to become successful in achieving goals and tasks?

   Yes _____
   No _____
   Undecided _____

REFLECTION

Reflection: Utilize this space to process all information you've discovered, learned and will apply from each section you've worked on today.

_____

_____

_____

_____

_____

_____

_____

_____

_____

_____

_____

_____

SECTION 11

Key points to ponder:
Knowledgeable- possessing or exhibiting knowledge, insight or understanding; intelligent; well-Informed, discerning; perceptive.
Keen- eager, enthusiastic and sharp.

Complete the following statement by inserting both key points to ponder where you believe it belongs.

In this life, there will be obstacles and trials that make achieving tasks and goals seem impossible. You become _____ when you allow yourself to experience and explore endless possibilities. Even the word impossible has possible in it, which is also an adjective, meaning a descriptive word that modifies or describes a noun or pronoun. Nouns are representations of a person, place, thing, concept or place, while a pronoun stands in for a noun. Although we may or may not like that life teaches us things via experiences, we can become _____ minded, resilient and vigilant even during troublesome times.

—Boldly,
Coach B

Insert your name here: _____

LESSON QUESTIONS

1. Create a timeline using the years provided to reflect the emotion experienced during this time. If you find that the listed emotion does not apply to your personal experience, name your own emotion.

   2020(anxiety) _____

   2021(contentment)_____

   2023(calm) _____

   2024(confusion) _____

365 on ME Questionnaire – Elaborate on each answer to the questionnaire.

1. Are there negative influences that prevent you from experiencing a lifestyle that offers freedom?

    Yes _____
    No _____
    Undecided _____

2. As a continuation from Question 1, are you willing to allow yourself to experience a life where you can be comfortable and free from negative influences?

    Yes _____
    No _____
    Undecided _____

REFLECTION

Reflection: Utilize this space to process all information you've discovered, learned and will apply from each section you've worked on today.

_____
_____
_____
_____
_____
_____
_____

SECTION 12

Key points to ponder:
Lighthearted- carefree, happy, without worry or anxiety.
Lambent- describing a soft, glowing light or gentle glow, indicating a peaceful and serene atmosphere.

Persistence | ˈnä-li-jə-bəl | —The quality or state of being persistent or tenacious.

LESSON QUESTIONS

1. Describe a time when you felt lighthearted and free.

   _____

   _____

   _____

2. How would you verbally express yourself when you are feeling lambent and radiant?

   _____

   _____

   _____

365 on ME Questionnaire - Elaborate on each answer to the questionnaire.

1. Do you experience moments when you just don't feel like being positive or thinking positively?

   Yes _____
   No _____
   Undecided _____

2. Are there people, places or circumstances that interfere with your ability to express your true feelings about a particular situation?

Yes _____
No _____
Undecided _____

REFLECTION

Reflection: Utilize this space to process all information you've discovered, learned and will apply from each section you've worked on today.

_____

_____

_____

_____

_____

_____

_____

_____

_____

_____

SECTION 13

Key points to ponder:
Magnetic- extremely beautiful or impressive.
Mindful- state of active open attention to the present.
Modest- unassuming or moderate in the estimation of one's abilities or achievements.

Manifestation | ˌma-nə-fə-ˈstā-shən |—The act, processor an instance of manifesting;bringing your desires to fruition.

HOW TO MANIFEST BY SHAKIRA MARIA

Complete your seven ways to manifest what you desire by following the examples listed for you.

- Decide what you want (ex. Freedom).
  _____

- Feel the energy of your desire (ex. Peace).
  _____

- Visualize your desire (ex. Living on a small island surrounded by nature).
  _____

- Release limiting beliefs (ex. I will have all that I desire to experience freedom).
  _____

- Believe in your ability to manifest (ex. I believe it, I feel it and so it shall be).
  _____

- Take inspired action (ex. No matter what, I will speak all things into existence).
  _____

- Allow the process to unfold (ex. By speaking and believing, I will experience what I desire).
  _____

LESSON QUESTIONS

1. List three to five things that you are currently manifesting in your life, and for each, list how you are demonstrating a modest spirit as things will come to fruition.

   _____

   _____

   _____

2. Complete the affirmation below by adding key points to ponder where you see fit.

   There's a life that I desire for myself. This life is imperfect yet beautifully flawed, sometimes unpredictable, but I will uphold myself in the most _____ manner and remain _____ and _____ so that I may attract positivity, peace and abundance.

   —Immeasurably 888
   Coach B,

   Insert your name here: _____

365 on ME Questionnaire – Elaborate on each answer to the questionnaire.

1. Do you truly believe in the power of manifestation?

   Yes _____
   No _____
   Undecided _____

2. Have you manifested something that never happened, and because of the results, you now doubt the power of manifestation?

   Yes _____
   No _____
   Undecided _____

REFLECTION

Reflection: Utilize this space to process all information you've discovered, learned and will apply from each section you've worked on today.

_____
_____
_____
_____
_____
_____
_____
_____
_____
_____

SECTION 14

Key points to ponder:
Noble- conveys a sense of high moral principles.
Nourishing- cultivating something to be healthy and grow and develop.
Nurturing- caring and supporting.

Motivation | ˌmō-tə-ˈvā-shən | —The general desire or willingness of someone to do something.

Complete the following by writing a positive word that starts with each letter and briefly describe how you will begin to demonstrate this in your life. Once you've completed this section, focus your attention on being intentional, and start utilizing your own tools which YOU have created to demonstrate the positive action.

M (EX. Mindful) - I will be conscious and mindful of my thoughts and actions.

M - _____

O - _____

T - _____

I - _____

V - _____

A - _____

T - _____

I - _____

O - _____

N - _____

LESSON QUESTIONS

1. What are two driving forces (not people) that motivate you to be the best person that you can be for yourself?

   _____

   _____

   _____

2. How can you assure that your ambition is parallel with noble intentions?

_____

_____

_____

3. What do you believe it takes for you to become motivated to complete difficult tasks while assuming other positions and titles that also allow you to be nourishing and nurturing to others?

_____

_____

_____

365 on ME Questionnaire – Elaborate on each answer to the questionnaire.

1. Do you depend or rely on a source or a person(s) to motivate you?

    Yes _____
    No _____
    Undecided _____

REFLECTION

Reflection: Utilize this space to process all information you've discovered, learned and will apply from each section you've worked on today.

_____

_____

_____

_____
_____
_____
_____
_____
_____
_____
_____

SECTION 14

Key points to ponder:
Optimistic- having a positive outlook on life.
Omnipotent- having unlimited power and authority.
Obliging- observant, paying attention.

Self-discipline | ˌself-ˈker | —The ability to control one's feelings to overcome one's weaknesses.

Quick note from the author:
Anything that you deem to be worthy deserves your full potential and attention. If you wish to prevail, you must show up for yourself and rely heavily on your own abilities without wavering.

—Unapologetically,
Coach B

LESSON QUESTIONS

1. List at least two ways that you practice discipline in your life and can be optimistic about this practice.

   _____

   _____

   _____

2. Values are the things you cherish the most in life whether they be your goals, priorities or identity. List the top three values held as demonstrated below. Be sure to stay true and authentic with yourself regardless of what you think others may or may not believe.

   Myself (Ex. I value my mental health.)

   _____

   Family (Ex. I value family time.)

   _____

   Friends (Ex. I value my relationship with my friends.)

   _____

   Society (Ex. I value open-mindedness in society.)

   _____

365 on ME Questionnaire – Elaborate on each answer to the questionnaire.

1. Are you a person that demonstrates optimism when making an unfavorable decision?

   Yes _____
   No _____
   Undecided _____

2. Do you believe others may confuse your optimism with arrogance?

   Yes ____
   No ____
   Undecided ____

3. Do you think it's important to be obliging?

   Yes ____
   No ____
   Undecided ____

REFLECTION

Reflection: Utilize this space to process all information you've discovered, learned and will apply from each section you've worked on today.

_____

_____

_____

_____

_____

_____

_____

_____

_____

SECTION 15

Key points to ponder:
Passionate- expressing intense emotions or interests.
Productive- a person's capability to do a lot of work.
Peaceful- signifying a state of calmness and tranquility.

Growth Part 2 | ˈgrōth |—The process of increasing in physical size.

PERSONAL GROWTH/REFLECTION

Over the past four years, I have experienced some seriously stressful and traumatic circumstances that were not self-inflicted (so I thought), yet I became the burden carrier because of what I allowed (my choice, right?). Initially, I was devastated and felt a little broken because I pondered,Why me ? Yep, I had the " Why me?" syndrome UNTIL I sought help. I had a therapist in the past, and she was wonderful, and it worked, and I applied the skills and rehabilitated myself by using the techniques plus continued aftercare. The help that I'm speaking of was from a life coach, Erin. I didn't need therapy at the time I needed life guidance from a free- spirited and transparent- styled coaching professional, and it is indeed what I received. I saw Erin for about six months, one to two times a week, and boy, did she work me (HAHA)! She gave me homework assignments each visit, and I was sure to complete all in totality as instructed. Considering I, too, am a certified life coach, I valued and respected her work as well as her expertise. Long story short, after I told Erin my story, she looked at me dead in my eyes and said, "Bianca, you are self-sabotaging." I immediately developed a dry lump in my throat,stared her back in her eyes and said, "WHAT!"—not in a disrespectful manner but out of shock. However, she was right, and I was unaware. Although I didn't know I was self-sabotaging, when she called me out on my stuff, I immediately started reflecting. I started writing the events and persons that I'd shared my story about per her instructions, and BOOM —I was,in fact, sabotaging myself. Fast forward to today (two and a half years later), I am now able to refine my energy when I encounter negativity. I have become more self-aware, and I noticed that once I stopped viewing things from the " Why me?" retrospective manner, the weight that I'd been carrying started to lighten ... and I no longer carry it. See, there's a lot of self-work to do even for a person who is pure and genuine. A lot of times, we blame the irrational behaviors displayed by others to overshadow our own imperfections. I started to focus more on myself,not so much on what others were doing or pain they'd inflicted upon me, and started taking accountability for my own stuff. That's when my life changed, my spirit was lighter and my soul was freed.

—Freedom Elevated,
Coach B

LESSON QUESTIONS

1. List ways in which you desire growth in each area of your life listed below.

    - Mentally-_____

    - Physically-_____

    - Emotionally-_____

    - Financially-_____

    - Spiritually-_____

2. Name three things that you are passionate about. How do these things contribute to your ability to grow?

_____

_____

_____

_____

_____

_____

365 on ME Questionnaire – Elaborate on each answer to the questionnaire.

1. Being true and authentic to yourself, are you a productive person who get things done without making excuses?

    Yes _____
    No _____
    Undecided _____

2. Have you allowed the actions of others to cause you to not have peaceful experiences?

    Yes _____
    No _____
    Undecided _____

REFLECTION

Reflection: Utilize this space to process all information you've discovered, learned and will apply from each section you've worked on today.

_____
_____
_____
_____
_____
_____
_____

SECTION 16

Key points to ponder:
Quick-witted- intelligent and good at thinking quickly.
Quotable- fit for or worth quoting.

Self-awareness | ˌself-ə-ˈwer-nəs |—An awareness of one's own personality or individuality.

LESSON QUESTIONS

1. Describe a time when you were self-aware and demonstrated the characteristic of quick-witted.

   _____

   _____

   _____

2. Identify two areas of your life in which you believe notable change is needed to become more self-aware.

   _____

   _____

   _____

365 on ME Questionnaire – Elaborate on each answer to the questionnaire.

1. Do you think it's important to be self-aware?

   Yes ——
   No ——
   Undecided ——

2. Would you acknowledge yourself to be a person that is worthy of your own words via quotable statements?

   Yes _____
   No _____
   Undecided _____

REFLECTION

Reflection: Utilize this space to process all information you've discovered, learned and will apply from each section you've worked on today.

_____

_____

_____

_____

_____

_____

_____

_____

_____

_____

_____

SECTION 17

Key points to ponder:
Radiating- emitting energy or light.
Radiance- beauty, happiness or good healthy glow.

Choosing | ˈchü-ziŋ | —An act of selecting or deciding when faced with two or more possibilities.

Quick note from the author:
I'm aware that choosing or making a decision is by far one of the most difficult things for a lot of people to do. If and when you find yourself in pickle or a position where you have no desire or ability to decide, use your intuition so that your decision isn't based on bias or a last minute quick deciding factor that could cause you unforeseen consequences, but allow your soul to approve whatever it is that you're faced with.

—Wise Up,
Coach B

LESSON QUESTIONS

1. Explain how you've experienced difficulties when making decisions and you were still able to produce a radiant spirit in lieu of your challenge.

   _____

   _____

   _____

2. Complete each phrase by expressing your ability to remain a radiating being even when you are in a dark place.

   R - Respect, responsibility and confidence are what I have, therefore

   _____

A - Authentic, self-driven and steadfast of my own choices, no matter what

_____

D - Decisive and aligned with the peace I have created regarding

_____

I - Immovable and unparalleled faith that keeps me

_____

A - Aligned, engaged and knowledgeable of the importance of making healthy choices that

_____

T - Thoughtful and tenacious- spirited, therefore I know that I will

_____

I - Impactful, strong and persistent because I know that

_____

N - Nourishing myself because I believe

_____

G - Gallant efforts that demonstrate my own ability to

_____

365 on ME Questionnaire – Elaborate on each answer to the questionnaire.

1. Are you a decisive person when it comes to making important decisions about your life?

   Yes _____
   No _____
   Undecided _____

2. When tasked to decide within a group, family or team, do you rely on other's input?

   Yes _____
   No _____
   Undecided _____

REFLECTION

Reflection: Utilize this space to process all information you've discovered, learned and will apply from each section you've worked on today.

_____

_____

_____

_____

_____

_____

_____

SECTION 18

Key points to ponder:
Secure- feeling safe and confident.
Strong- resilient spirit.
Self-assured- confident and with a great sense of assurance.

Balance | ˈba-lən(t)s | —An even distribution of weight, enabling someone or something to remain upright and steady.

Quick note from the author:
Living in a society where we're constantly being told what we should do, what religion or spiritual organization we should engage in, how much we should or shouldn't work or eat, or when we should or shouldn't travel can be annoyingly exhausting. The good news is that we can choose to change this narrative. Now, some would say that we break the rules and even go to the extent to call us rebels or mavericks. I don't know about you, friend, but I'm okay with being called both because here's the thing: A rebel is defined as one who RISES in opposition. Why does this have to be a negative thing? A maverick is simply a person who doesn't necessarily believe that some rules apply to them. Why does this have to be a negative thing?

According to the first amendment, as a citizen of the United States (I'm sure these amendment rights may not reference to others in different countries, but I believe everyone has their own voice and should be able to exercise their own human rights no matter where they are in the world), a person is allowed "freedom of speech, religion, press, assembly and petition." The point is, YOU can choose balance in your life whether that pertains to work, school, personal life, relationships and so forth. If you desire to go to college, become a wife/husband and/or have a child, you're allowed to assume all roles — and if you're able to balance all, go for it!

LESSON QUESTIONS

1. Using the first letter of the word balance, create a positive statement or quote that relates to your belief and thoughts when it comes to balance. An example has been provided for you to use as a guide.

    B - Boldly I stand amid adversity, and I will still create balance in my life that works for me.

A - Abiding respect towards others while upholding my own dignity and rights is what I stand for.

L - Loving myself and creating a lifestyle that I desire is vital to my mental and emotional well-being.

A - Abundance, growth, patience, and grace is what I'm speaking over my life.

N - Nonpareil and unmovable, I will choose and decide what works for me in my life unapologetically.

C - Confidently I will work, play and do all the things that I desire because I know that I will balance it all.

E - Enthusiastically, I, too, am optimistic about my desires; therefore, I will continue to create a lifestyle that demonstrates FREEDOM!

B - _____

A - _____

L - _____

A - _____

N - _____

C - _____

E - _____

2. Fill in the blanks, using each key point to ponder.

Although my life is imperfect with balance right now, I am _____ and optimistic that with continuous self-work and dedication, I will create a lifestyle that demonstrates my ability to operate in my higher self without doubt or insecurities. I also believe that I am _____ and _____; therefore, I will preserve even when faced with challenges. Challenges no longer have power or authority over my life.

365 on ME Questionnaire – Elaborate on each answer to the questionnaire.

1. Do you find it difficult to create balance in your life due to an overwhelming job or personal family matter?

   Yes _____
   No _____
   Undecided _____

2. Will you decide to choose yourself when you feel that someone or something impedes your ability to do the things that you desire to do in your life?

   Yes _____
   No _____
   Undecided _____

REFLECTION

Reflection: Utilize this space to process all information you've discovered, learned and will apply from each section you've worked on today.

_____
_____
_____
_____
_____
_____
_____

SECTION 19

Key points to ponder:
Thoughtful- absorbed in or involving thought showing consideration.
Tactful- saying the right thing (considerate).
Teachable- eager to learn and grow.
Resilience- the capacity to recover quickly from difficulties; toughness.

LESSON QUESTIONS

1. Share a time when you demonstrated resilience even though the situation caused you pain and suffering.

   _____

   _____

2. When you have experienced moments in which you did not acquire the accuracy of information? Express how and if you were teachable.

   _____

   _____

365 on ME Questionnaire - Elaborate on each answer to the questionnaire.

1. When or if you know that you are "right" or honest about something, is it challenging for you to remain tactful although other's point of view or decision differs from yours?

   Yes _____
   No _____
   Undecided _____

2. During a disagreement with someone that you care about and respect, do you find it difficult to be thoughtful of that person's feelings because you feel you have expressed logic, whereas they are combative and/or display disregard for your feelings and thoughts?

Yes ____
No ____
Undecided ____

REFLECTION

Reflection: Utilize this space to process all information you've discovered, learned and will apply from each section you've worked on today.

_____
_____
_____
_____
_____
_____
_____
_____
_____
_____

SECTION 20

Key points to ponder:
Unique- kind, distinct, or remarkable.
Undefeated- showing incredible determination.
Unparalleled- unmatched, no equal, unmatched in quality or significance.

Change | ˈchānj |—The ability to make someone or something different; alter or modify.

LESSON QUESTIONS

1. What areas in your life demand change? How will you begin to make changes in these areas?

   _____

2. Describe what makes you unique in the areas listed below.

   - Career/work _____

   - Personal relationships (significant other/spouse/friend) _____

   - Physical (exercise/workout) _____

   - Financially (savings/income) _____

3. Explain how you can sustain yourself during a challenging situation that causes you stress and grief.

   _____

   _____

   _____

   _____

365 on ME Questionnaire ‑ Elaborate on each answer to the questionnaire.

1. Do you allow doubt, previous disappointments, or unsuccessful attempts to cause you to feel undefeated?

    Yes _____
    No _____
    Undecided _____

2. In your past, have you experienced situations where you felt that you were undefeated when your patience and tolerance were tested?

    Yes _____
    No _____
    Undecided _____

REFLECTION

Reflection: Utilize this space to process all information you've discovered, learned and will apply from each section you've worked on today.

_____
_____
_____
_____
_____
_____
_____

SECTION 21

Key points to ponder:
Versatile- adaptable all around, flexible.
Vibrant-full of life and energy, brave and courageous.
Vigilant- watchful, alert and attentive.

Serenity | sə-ˈre-nə-tē | —The state of being calm, peaceful and untroubled.

TASK: RELAX

There comes a time in this life when we must learn that relaxation, quiet time and peace are necessary. Learning how to quiet the mind can be a huge task that seems impossible. Sometimes, this means you will need to unplug from people, places and things. Turn the phone off or on put it on "do not disturb,"no music, no TV , and allow solitude to befriend you. A person who's able to be alone is indeed a powerful being. Are you able to just relax?

~Peacefully Relaxing,
Coach B

LESSON QUESTIONS

1. What do you do when life is busy and noisy, and you find it difficult to find peace and quiet?

_____
_____
_____
_____

2. Although life seems to have its way of dealing us a hand that we don't believe in or think we deserve at times, how do you remain vigilant and focused? If you need to work on this area, in what ways do you plan on making a change so that you can become vigilant and focused?

_____

_____

_____

_____

365 on ME Questionnaire – Elaborate on each answer to the questionnaire.

1. Are there times in life when you feel that you are in a dark place, and it's hard for you to have as vibrant a spirit as you had before?

    Yes _____
    No _____
    Undecided _____

2. Do you believe that being able to be versatile and flexible could help to promote a successful and healthy lifestyle for yourself?

    Yes _____
    No _____
    Undecided _____

REFLECTION

Reflection: Utilize this space to process all information you've discovered, learned and will apply from each section you've worked on today.

_____

_____

_____

_____

_____

_____

_____

_____

_____

_____

SECTION 22

Key points to ponder:
Wholesome- promoting health and well-being.
Well-balanced- successful and stable in several areas of life.

Mindfulness | ˈmīn(d)-fəl-nəs |—The quality or state of being conscious or aware of something.

SIX POSITIVE MINDFULNESS AFFIRMATIONS

I am safe and secure.

I am not my circumstances.

My mind is resilient.

I am alive and well.

I am not my thoughts.

I am grounded and steadfast.

Repeat the aforementioned positive mindfulness affirmations. Create six of your own affirmations that differ from the previous ones.

1. _____

2. _____

3. _____

4. _____

5. _____

6. _____

LESSON QUESTIONS

1. Because you are positioning yourself to be strong or stronger at heart and mind, share two important concepts of wholesomeness and how you will demonstrate it in your life.

_____

_____

_____

_____

_____

_____

_____

2. Describe what you believe it means to be well-balanced in your life. What areas (personal, professional, etc.) do you believe contribute to your ability to be well-balanced?

_____

_____

_____

_____

_____

365 on ME Questionnaire – Elaborate on each answer to the questionnaire.

1. Do you know for sure that you are not doing the self-work that's required to get you to a comfortable place in life where you can become wholesome?

    Yes _____
    No _____
    Undecided _____

2. Are there people, places or situations that are distractions and don't promote the well-balanced lifestyle that you desire?
    Yes _____
    No _____
    Undecided _____

REFLECTION

Reflection: Utilize this space to process all information you've discovered, learned and will apply from each section you've worked on today.

_____

_____

_____

_____

_____

_____

_____

_____

_____

_____

SECTION 23

Key points to ponder:
Yielding- giving way under pressure.
Yare- active, quick, ready and prepared.

Reward | ri-'wȯrd | —Anything given in recognition of one's service, effort or achievement.

REWARD AFFIRMATION

R - Realign your focus.

E - Establish an ambition that requires you to always show up as your best self.

W - Willingly avoid and decline people that choose not to show up as their best self.

A - Acknowledge your own strength, and do not wait for others to give you flowers.

R - Revisit your past only to remind yourself that you do not have to go back there.

D - Discipline yourself so that you can achieve your goals and stay consistent and precise.

Redo the Reward Affirmation using at least one of the key points to ponder in each sentence.

R - _____

E - _____

W - _____

A - _____

R - _____

D - _____

LESSON QUESTIONS

1. Share a time in the past when you have rewarded yourself non-monetarily(i.e. talking a peaceful walk, reading a book, meditating, etc.). Plan a time in the future when you will reward yourself non-monetarily.

   _____
   _____
   _____
   _____
   _____
   _____
   _____

2. In what ways have you yielded in your life, mentally, emotionally, financially and spiritually?

   _____
   _____
   _____
   _____
   _____
   _____
   _____

365 on ME Questionnaire – Elaborate on each answer to the questionnaire.

1. Have there been times in your life when you knew that you had the ability to display a yare spirit of determination, and you failed to do so?

    Yes ____
    No ____
    Undecided ____

2. In approximately two years from today, do you believe that you will have evolved and become more aware of your talents and skills?

    Yes ____
    No ____
    Undecided ____

REFLECTION

Reflection: Utilize this space to process all information you've discovered, learned and will apply from each section you've worked on today.

_____
_____
_____
_____
_____
_____
_____

SECTION 24

Key points to ponder:
Zestful- filled with enthusiasm, vigor and energy.
Zen- calm and attentiveness.
Zoetic- relating to or of life, or living vital.

Self-disciplined | ˌself-ˈdi-sə-plənd | —The ability to control one's feelings and overcome one's weaknesses; the ability to pursue what one thinks is right despite temptations to abandon it.

Quick note from the author:
In completion of the first half of this book, I challenge you to reflect on your life over the past 30 days. Have you made notable contributions and changes to your mental or physical wellness? Have you started a new and positive regimen? Have you been intentional in your self-discovery journey as far as realizing that you don't walk, talk or do the same as you used to because you're evolving? Have you engulfed yourself in new horizons and interests and discovered tasks and skills you never knew you'd possess? Yes, I know that it is a lot to take in. However, learning to pace yourself and practice balance will help you to not only process these lessons but also relax in knowing that in due time, you will get YOURSELF to where you desire to be if YOU DESIRE to be!

—Immersive Intent,
Coach B

LESSON QUESTIONS

1. In your own words, what does it mean to be self-disciplined?

   _____

   _____

   _____

   _____

2. In what ways have you demonstrated the following key points to ponder?

- Zestful - _____
  _____

- Zen - _____
  _____

- Zoetic - _____
  _____

3. Considering new educational guidance that this book has provided thus far, acknowledge, express and define the top three takeaways regarding overall wellness.

   1._____
   _____

   2._____
   _____

   3._____
   _____

365 on ME Questionnaire - Elaborate on each answer to the questionnaire.

1. Have you displayed self-discipline in your life when you were in dire need?

   Yes _____
   No _____
   Undecided _____

2. Are you truly committed to becoming a better version of who you are, who you've been and who you're used to being?

   Yes _____
   No _____
   Undecided _____

REFLECTION

Reflection: Utilize this space to process all information you've discovered, learned and will apply from each section you've worked on today.

_____
_____
_____
_____
_____
_____
_____
_____
_____
_____
_____

TAKE THIS TIME TO PAUSE ON PURPOSE

Please do not proceed to the next section of this book until you have allowed yourself time to take an intentional break. The author recommends taking three days off from reading and interactive work to reflect, release and relax. The next section will prepare you for more intentional self-work. Please pace yourself.

—Intensively Resting,
Coach B

On your mark, get set, LET'S GOOOOOOOOOOOOOOOOOOOOOO!!!

WELCOME LETTER

Greetings friends and family,

I am very proud of you for getting this far. Please understand that this book has a variety of information, and sometimes, if you do not create balance in between your lessons, you may experience information overload and burnout. While this is not the author's intention, she strongly encourages you to take minor breaks even throughout the first section so that you can come to a new lesson fresh and ready to press play. With that being said, after each section of this second portion of the book, the author recommends a two-day break in between every lesson. This time should be utilized to practice the skills provided and self-observation. You will find a self-observation section in each new lesson, which requires you to reflect on the previous lesson and provide responses to that lesson only. I hope that you are fired up and ready to continue your journey of self-work.

—Flowers Watered,
Coach B

Welcome to section two of Self-Work A-Z

WELCOME TO SECTION TWO OF SELF-WORK A-Z

SELF-OBSERVATION

Describe how you displayed skills of the previous lesson.

Elevation - Describe how you have demonstrated elevation in your life over the past 30 days.

_____

_____

_____

CALMNESS

Describe how you have demonstrated calmness in your life over the past 30 days.

_____

_____

_____

RELAXATION

Describe how you have demonstrated relaxation in your life over the past 30 days.

_____

_____

_____

Whether we choose to identify and/or recognize defaults, roadblocks, hurdles and U-turns in life, they will surface from time to time. Even in the midst of thriving and making progress, there will be inconveniences and life's circumstances that happen and sometimes set us back, BUT they allow us to learn from these situations and make better and different decisions while learning new ways to balance life. The key is holding ourselves accountable and learning to recognize what it is that's keeping us from becoming who and what we desire to be and learning how to rid the waste. In this section, you will be challenged to answer three very important questions so that you can and WILL get to the root of the problem and rid the waste. You may write your answers out, or you can answer these questions aloud. Please see the example below.

QUESTIONS TO PONDER

1. Does this situation, person or thing contribute to my overall mental well-being?
2. What am I losing if I decide no longer to engage in this behavior/activity?
3. What are 1-3 realistic questions to ponder when making decisions to move forward in life?

Example: Hindrance: An ex who doesn't see their own flaws and refuses to take accountability. **Allowing this person to stay in my life without noticeable desires to elevate.**

Example: Rid The waste: Mark a date that you choose to free yourself of this situation, person or thing that's holding you back from moving forward in life. (**Date: 10/11/2024, Person/Situation: John-break-up**)

ELEVATION

Hindrance: _____

Rid the waste: _____

CALMNESS

Hindrance: _____

Rid the waste: _____

RELAXATION

Hindrance: _____

Rid the waste: _____

SELF-OBSERVATION

Describe how you displayed skills of the previous lesson.

_____

_____

_____

MANIFESTATION

Describe how you have demonstrated manifestation in your life over the past 30 days.

_____

_____

_____

SELF-ASSURANCE

Describe how you have demonstrated self-assurance in your life over the past 30 days.

_____

_____

_____

PEACE

Describe how you have demonstrated peace in your life over the past 30 days.

_____

_____

_____

Whether we choose to identify and/or recognize defaults, roadblocks, hurdles and U-turns in life, they will surface from time to time. Even in the midst of thriving and making progress, there will be inconveniences and life's circumstances that happen and sometimes set us back, BUT they allow us to learn from these situations and make better and different decisions while learning new ways to balance life. The key is holding ourselves accountable and learning to recognize what it is that's keeping us from becoming who and what we desire to be and learning how to rid the waste. In this section, you will be challenged to answer three very important questions so that you can and WILL get to the root of the problem and rid the waste. You may write your answers out, or you can answer these questions aloud. Please see the example below. Please utilize examples in the following sections.

QUESTIONS TO PONDER

1. Does this situation, person or thing contribute to my overall mental well-being?
2. What am I losing if I decide no longer to engage in this behavior/activity?
3. What are 1-3 realistic questions to ponder when making decisions to move forward in life?

MANIFESTATION

Hindrance: _____

Rid the waste: _____

SELF-ASSURANCE

Hindrance: _____

Rid the waste: _____

PEACE

Hindrance: _____

Rid the waste: _____

SELF-OBSERVATION

Describe how you displayed skills of the previous lesson.

_____

_____

_____

HEALING

Describe how you have demonstrated healing in your life over the past 30 days.

_____

_____

_____

COMFORT

Describe how you have demonstrated comfort in your life over the past 30 days.

_____

_____

_____

DIGNITY

Describe how you have demonstrated dignity in your life over the past 30 days.

_____

_____

_____

Whether we choose to identify and/or recognize defaults, roadblocks, hurdles and U-turns in life, they will surface from time to time. Even in the midst of thriving and making progress, there will be inconveniences and life's circumstances that happen and sometimes set us back, BUT they allow us to learn from these situations and make better and different decisions while learning new ways to balance life. The key is holding ourselves accountable and learning to recognize what it is that's keeping us from becoming who and what we desire to be and learning how to rid the waste. In this section, you will be challenged to answer three very important questions so that you can and WILL get to the root of the problem and rid the waste. You may write your answers out, or you can answer these questions aloud. Please see the example below. Please utilize examples in the following sections.

QUESTIONS TO PONDER

1. Does this situation, person or thing contribute to my overall mental well-being?
2. What am I losing if I decide no longer to engage in this behavior/activity?
3. What are 1-3 realistic questions to ponder when making decisions to move forward in life?

HEALING

Hindrance: _____

Rid the waste: _____

COMFORT

Hindrance: _____

Rid the waste: _____

DIGNITY

Hindrance: _____

Rid the waste: _____

SELF-OBSERVATION

Describe how you displayed skills of the previous lesson.

_____

_____

_____

SELF-ADMIRATION

Describe how you have demonstrated Self-admiration in your life over the past 30 days.

_____

_____

_____

BEAUTY

Describe how you have demonstrated beauty in your life over the past 30 days.

_____

_____

_____

COURAGE

Describe how you have demonstrated courage in your life over the past 30 days.

_____

_____

_____

Whether we choose to identify and/or recognize defaults, roadblocks, hurdles and U-turns in life, they will surface from time to time. Even in the midst of thriving and making progress, there will be inconveniences and life's circumstances that happen and sometimes set us back, BUT they allow us to learn from these situations and make better and different decisions while learning new ways to balance life. The key is holding ourselves accountable and learning to recognize what it is that's keeping us from becoming who and what we desire to be and learning how to rid the waste. In this section, you will be challenged to answer three very important questions so that you can and WILL get to the root of the problem and rid the waste. You may write your answers out, or you can answer these questions aloud. Please see the example below. Please utilize examples in the following sections.

QUESTIONS TO PONDER

1. Does this situation, person or thing contribute to my overall mental well-being?

2. What am I losing if I decide no longer to engage in this behavior/activity?

3. What are 1-3 realistic questions to ponder when making decisions to move forward in life?

SELF-ADMIRATION

Hindrance: _____

Rid the waste: _____

BEAUTY

Hindrance: _____

Rid the waste: _____

COURAGE

Hindrance: _____

Rid the waste: _____

SELF-OBSERVATION

Describe how you displayed skills of the previous lesson.

_____

_____

_____

INSPIRATION

Describe how you have demonstrated inspiration in your life over the past 30 days.

_____

_____

_____

DETERMINATION

Describe how you have demonstrated determination in your life over the past 30 days.

_____

_____

_____

PERSEVERANCE

Describe how you have demonstrated perseverance in your life over the past 30 days.

_____

_____

_____

Whether we choose to identify and/or recognize defaults, roadblocks, hurdles and U-turns in life, they will surface from time to time. Even in the midst of thriving and making progress, there will be inconveniences and life's circumstances that happen and sometimes set us back, BUT they allow us to learn from these situations and make better and different decisions while learning new ways to balance life. The key is holding ourselves accountable and learning to recognize what it is that's keeping us from becoming who and what we desire to be and learning how to rid the waste. In this section, you will be challenged to answer three very important questions so that you can and WILL get to the root of the problem and rid the waste. You may write your answers out, or you can answer these questions aloud. Please see the example below. Please utilize examples in the following sections.

QUESTIONS TO PONDER

1. Does this situation, person or thing contribute to my overall mental well-being?
2. What am I losing if I decide no longer to engage in this behavior/activity?
3. What are 1-3 realistic questions to ponder when making decisions to move forward in life?

INSPIRATION

Hindrance: _____

Rid the waste: _____

DETERMINATION

Hindrance: _____

Rid the waste: _____

PERSEVERANCE

Hindrance: _____

Rid the waste: _____

SELF-OBSERVATION

Describe how you displayed skills of the previous lesson.

_____

_____

_____

UNDERSTANDING

Describe how you have demonstrated understanding in your life over the past 30 days.

_____

_____

_____

SELF-CONCEPT

Describe how you have demonstrated self-concept in your life over the past 30 days.

_____

_____

_____

WISDOM

Describe how you have demonstrated wisdom in your life over the past 30 days.

_____

_____

_____

Whether we choose to identify and/or recognize defaults, roadblocks, hurdles and U-turns in life, they will surface from time to time. Even in the midst of thriving and making progress, there will be inconveniences and life's circumstances that happen and sometimes set us back, BUT they allow us to learn from these situations and make better and different decisions while learning new ways to balance life. The key is holding ourselves accountable and learning to recognize what it is that's keeping us from becoming who and what we desire to be and learning how to rid the waste. In this section, you will be challenged to answer three very important questions so that you can and WILL get to the root of the problem and rid the waste. You may write your answers out, or you can answer these questions aloud. Please see the example below. Please utilize examples in the following sections.

QUESTIONS TO PONDER

1. Does this situation, person or thing contribute to my overall mental well-being?
2. What am I losing if I decide no longer to engage in this behavior/activity?
3. What are 1-3 realistic questions to ponder when making decisions to move forward in life?

SELF-OBSERVATION

Describe how you displayed skills of the previous lesson.

___

___

___

KNOWLEDGE

Describe how you have demonstrated understanding in your life over the past 30 days.

___

___

___

RESPONSIBILITY

Describe how you have demonstrated responsibility in your life over the past 30 days.

___

___

___

MINDSET

Describe how you have demonstrated mindset in your life over the past 30 days.

___

___

___

Whether we choose to identify and/or recognize defaults, roadblocks, hurdles and U-turns in life, they will surface from time to time. Even in the midst of thriving and making progress, there will be inconveniences and life's circumstances that happen and sometimes set us back, BUT they allow us to learn from these situations and make better and different decisions while learning new ways to balance life. The key is holding ourselves accountable and learning to recognize what it is that's keeping us from becoming who and what we desire to be and learning how to rid the waste. In this section, you will be challenged to answer three very important questions so that you can and WILL get to the root of the problem and rid the waste. You may write your answers out, or you can answer these questions aloud. Please see the example below. Please utilize examples in the following sections.

QUESTIONS TO PONDER

1. Does this situation, person or thing contribute to my overall mental well-being?
2. What am I losing if I decide no longer to engage in this behavior/activity?
3. What are 1-3 realistic questions to ponder when making decisions to move forward in life?

KNOWLEDGE

Hindrance: _____

Rid the waste: _____

RESPONSIBILITY

Hindrance: _____

Rid the waste: _____

MINDSET

Hindrance: _____

Rid the waste: _____

SELF-OBSERVATION

Describe how you displayed skills of the previous lesson.

_____
_____
_____

ACCOUNTABILITY

Describe how you have demonstrated accountability in your life over the past 30 days.

_____
_____
_____

REALIZATION

Describe how you have demonstrated realization in your life over the past 30 days.

_____
_____
_____

EMPATHY

Describe how you have demonstrated empathy in your life over the past 30 days.

_____
_____
_____

Whether we choose to identify and/or recognize defaults, roadblocks, hurdles and U-turns in life, they will surface from time to time. Even in the midst of thriving and making progress, there will be inconveniences and life's circumstances that happen and sometimes set us back, BUT they allow us to learn from these situations and make better and different decisions while learning new ways to balance life. The key is holding ourselves accountable and learning to recognize what it is that's keeping us from becoming who and what we desire to be and learning how to rid the waste. In this section, you will be challenged to answer three very important questions so that you can and WILL get to the root of the problem and rid the waste. You may write your answers out, or you can answer these questions aloud. Please see the example below. Please utilize examples in the following sections.

QUESTIONS TO PONDER

1. Does this situation, person or thing contribute to my overall mental well-being?
2. What am I losing if I decide no longer to engage in this behavior/activity?
3. What are 1-3 realistic questions to ponder when making decisions to move forward in life?

ACCOUNTABILITY

Hindrance: _____

Rid the waste: _____

REALIZATION

Hindrance: _____

Rid the waste: _____

EMPATH

Hindrance: _____

Rid the waste: _____

Whether we choose to identify and/or recognize defaults, roadblocks, hurdles and U-turns in life, they will surface from time to time. Even in the midst of thriving and making progress, there will be inconveniences and life's circumstances that happen and sometimes set us back, BUT they allow us to learn from these situations and make better and different decisions while learning new ways to balance life. The key is holding ourselves accountable and learning to recognize what it is that's keeping us from becoming who and what we desire to be and learning how to rid the waste. In this section, you will be challenged to answer three very important questions so that you can and WILL get to the root of the problem and rid the waste. You may write your answers out, or you can answer these questions aloud. Please see the example below. Please utilize examples in the following sections.

QUESTIONS TO PONDER

1. Does this situation, person or thing contribute to my overall mental well-being?
2. What am I losing if I decide no longer to engage in this behavior/activity?
3. 1 - 3 realistic questions to ponder when making decisions to move forward in life.

SELF-OBSERVATION

Describe how you displayed skills of the previous lesson.

_____

_____

_____

WELLNESS

Describe how you have demonstrated wellness in your life over the past 30 days.

_____

_____

_____

PURPOSE

Describe how you have demonstrated purpose in your life over the past 30 days.

_____

_____

_____

SELF-EDUCATE

Describe how you have demonstrated self-education in your life over the past 30 days.

_____

_____

_____

Whether we choose to identify and/or recognize defaults, roadblocks, hurdles and U-turns in life, they will surface from time to time. Even in the midst of thriving and making progress, there will be inconveniences and life's circumstances that happen and sometimes set us back, BUT they allow us to learn from these situations and make better and different decisions while learning new ways to balance life. The key is holding ourselves accountable and learning to recognize what it is that's keeping us from becoming who and what we desire to be and learning how to rid the waste. In this section, you will be challenged to answer three very important questions so that you can and WILL get to the root of the problem and rid the waste. You may write your answers out, or you can answer these questions aloud. Please see the example below. Please utilize examples in the following sections.

QUESTIONS TO PONDER

1. Does this situation, person or thing contribute to my overall mental well-being?
2. What am I losing if I decide no longer to engage in this behavior/activity?
3. What are 1-3 realistic questions to ponder when making decisions to move forward in life?

WELLNESS

Hindrance: _____

Rid the waste: _____

PURPOSE

Hindrance: _____

Rid the waste: _____

SELF-EDUCATE

Hindrance: _____

Rid the waste: _____

SELF-OBSERVATION

Describe how you displayed skills of the previous lesson.

_____

_____

_____

BOLDNESS

Describe how you have demonstrated boldness in your life over the past 30 days.

_____

_____

_____

EVALUATION

Describe how you have demonstrated evaluation in your life over the past 30 days.

_____

_____

_____

SELF-DISCOVERY

Describe how you have demonstrated self-discovery in your life over the past 30 days.

_____

_____

_____

ATTITUDE

Describe how you have demonstrated attitude in your life over the past 30 days.

_____

_____

_____

Whether we choose to identify and/or recognize defaults, roadblocks, hurdles and U-turns in life, they will surface from time to time. Even in the midst of thriving and making progress, there will be inconveniences and life's circumstances that happen and sometimes set us back, BUT they allow us to learn from these situations and make better and different decisions while learning new ways to balance life. The key is holding ourselves accountable and learning to recognize what it is that's keeping us from becoming who and what we desire to be and learning how to rid the waste. In this section, you will be challenged to answer three very important questions so that you can and WILL get to the root of the problem and rid the waste. You may write your answers out, or you can answer these questions aloud. Please see the example below. Please utilize examples in the following sections.

QUESTIONS TO PONDER

1. Does this situation, person or thing contribute to my overall mental well-being?
2. What am I losing if I decide no longer to engage in this behavior/activity?
3. What are 1-3 realistic questions to ponder when making decisions to move forward in life?

BOLDNESS

Hindrance: _____

Rid the waste: _____

EVALUATION

Hindrance: _____

Rid the waste: _____

SELF-DISCOVERY

Hindrance: _____

Rid the waste: _____

ATTITUDE

Hindrance: _____

Rid the waste: _____

SELF-OBSERVATION

Describe how you displayed skills of the previous lesson.

_____

_____

_____

SELF-INVESTMENT

Describe how you have demonstrated self-investment in your life over the past 30 days.

_____

_____

_____

POTENTIAL

Describe how you have demonstrated potential in your life over the past 30 days.

_____

_____

_____

RENEW

Describe how you have demonstrated renewal in your life over the past 30 days.

_____

_____

_____

FIERCE

Describe how you have demonstrated fierceness in your life over the past 30 days.

_____

_____

_____

INSIGHT

Describe how you have demonstrated insight in your life over the past 30 days.

_____

_____

_____

Whether we choose to identify and/or recognize defaults, roadblocks, hurdles and U-turns in life, they will surface from time to time. Even in the midst of thriving and making progress, there will be inconveniences and life's circumstances that happen and sometimes set us back, BUT they allow us to learn from these situations and make better and different decisions while learning new ways to balance life. The key is holding ourselves accountable and learning to recognize what it is that's keeping us from becoming who and what we desire to be and learning how to rid the waste. In this section, you will be challenged to answer three very important questions so that you can and WILL get to the root of the problem and rid the waste. You may write your answers out, or you can answer these questions aloud. Please see the example below. Please utilize examples in the following sections.

QUESTIONS TO PONDER

1. Does this situation, person or thing contribute to my overall mental well-being?
2. What am I losing if I decide no longer to engage in this behavior/activity?
3. What are 1-3 realistic questions to ponder when making decisions to move forward in life?

POTENTIAL

Hindrance: _____

Rid the waste: _____

RENEW

Hindrance: _____

Rid the waste: _____

FIERCE

Hindrance: _____

Rid the waste: _____

INSIGHT

Hindrance: _____

Rid the waste: _____

SELF-OBSERVATION

Describe how you displayed skills of the previous lesson.

_____

_____

_____

ENERGY

Describe how you have demonstrated energy in your life over the past 30 days.

_____

_____

_____

AMBITION

Describe how you have demonstrated ambition in your life over the past 30 days.

_____

_____

_____

MEDITATION

Describe how you have demonstrated meditation in your life over the past 30 days.

_____

_____

_____

Whether we choose to identify and/or recognize defaults, roadblocks, hurdles and U-turns in life, they will surface from time to time. Even in the midst of thriving and making progress, there will be inconveniences and life's circumstances that happen and sometimes set us back, BUT they allow us to learn from these situations and make better and different decisions while learning new ways to balance life. The key is holding ourselves accountable and learning to recognize what it is that's keeping us from becoming who and what we desire to be and learning how to rid the waste. In this section, you will be challenged to answer three very important questions so that you can and WILL get to the root of the problem and rid the waste. You may write your answers out, or you can answer these questions aloud. Please see the example below. Please utilize examples in the following sections.

QUESTIONS TO PONDER

1. Does this situation, person or thing contribute to my overall mental well-being?
2. What am I losing if I decide no longer to engage in this behavior/activity?
3. What are 1-3 realistic questions to ponder when making decisions to move forward in life?

ENERGY

Hindrance: _____

Rid the waste: _____

AMBITION

Hindrance: _____

Rid the waste: _____

MEDITATION

Hindrance: _____

Rid the waste: _____

SELF-OBSERVATION

Describe how you displayed skills of the previous lesson.

_____

_____

_____

CRITICAL THINKING

Describe how you have demonstrated critical thinking in your life over the past 30 days.

_____

_____

_____

INFLUENCE

Describe how you have demonstrated influence in your life over the past 30 days.

_____

_____

_____

REEVALUATE-REEVALUATION

Describe how you have demonstrated reevaluation in your life over the past 30 days.

_____

_____

_____

EXPLORE/EXPLORATION

Describe how you have demonstrated exploration in your life over the past 30 days.

_____

_____

_____

Whether we choose to identify and/or recognize defaults, roadblocks, hurdles and U-turns in life, they will surface from time to time. Even in the midst of thriving and making progress, there will be inconveniences and life's circumstances that happen and sometimes set us back, BUT they allow us to learn from these situations and make better and different decisions while learning new ways to balance life. The key is holding ourselves accountable and learning to recognize what it is that's keeping us from becoming who and what we desire to be and learning how to rid the waste. In this section, you will be challenged to answer three very important questions so that you can and WILL get to the root of the problem and rid the waste. You may write your answers out, or you can answer these questions aloud. Please see the example below. Please utilize examples in the following sections.

QUESTIONS TO PONDER

1. Does this situation, person or thing contribute to my overall mental well-being?
2. What am I losing if I decide no longer to engage in this behavior/activity?
3. What are 1-3 realistic questions to ponder when making decisions to move forward in life?

CRITICAL THINKING

Hindrance: _____

Rid the waste: _____

INFLUENCE

Hindrance: _____

Rid the waste: _____

REEVALUATE/REEVALUATION

Hindrance: _____

Rid the waste: _____

EXPLORE/EXPLORATION

Hindrance: _____

Rid the waste: _____

SELF-OBSERVATION

Describe how you displayed skills of the previous lesson.

_____

_____

_____

MENTALITY

Describe how you have demonstrated mental capacity in your life over the past 30 days.

_____

_____

_____

VENTURE

Describe how you have demonstrated venture in your life over the past 30 days.

_____

_____

_____

POWER

Describe how you have demonstrated power in your life over the past 30 days.

_____

_____

_____

SELF- RESPECT

Describe how you have demonstrated self-respect in your life over the past 30 days.

_____

_____

_____

Whether we choose to identify and/or recognize defaults, roadblocks, hurdles and U-turns in life, they will surface from time to time. Even in the midst of thriving and making progress, there will be inconveniences and life's circumstances that happen and sometimes set us back, BUT they allow us to learn from these situations and make better and different decisions while learning new ways to balance life. The key is holding ourselves accountable and learning to recognize what it is that's keeping us from becoming who and what we desire to be and learning how to rid the waste. In this section, you will be challenged to answer three very important questions so that you can and WILL get to the root of the problem and rid the waste. You may write your answers out, or you can answer these questions aloud. Please see the example below. Please utilize examples in the following sections.

QUESTIONS TO PONDER

1. Does this situation, person or thing contribute to my overall mental well-being?
2. What am I losing if I decide no longer to engage in this behavior/activity?
3. What are 1-3 realistic questions to ponder when making decisions to move forward in life?

MENTALITY

Hindrance: _____

Rid the waste: _____

VENTURE

Hindrance: _____

Rid the waste: _____

POWER

Hindrance: _____

Rid the waste: _____

SELF-RESPECT

Hindrance: _____

Rid the waste: _____

SELF-OBSERVATION

Describe how you displayed skills of the previous lesson.

_____

_____

_____

FEEL(INGS)

Describe how you have demonstrated feel (ings) in your life over the past 30 days.

_____

_____

_____

COMMITMENT

Describe how you have demonstrated commitment in your life over the past 30 days.

_____

_____

_____

ABILITY

Describe how you have demonstrated ability in your life over the past 30 days.

_____

_____

_____

EVOLUTION

Describe how you have demonstrated evolution in your life over the past 30 days.

_____

_____

_____

Whether we choose to identify and/or recognize defaults, roadblocks, hurdles and U-turns in life, they will surface from time to time. Even in the midst of thriving and making progress, there will be inconveniences and life's circumstances that happen and sometimes set us back, BUT they allow us to learn from these situations and make better and different decisions while learning new ways to balance life. The key is holding ourselves accountable and learning to recognize what it is that's keeping us from becoming who and what we desire to be and learning how to rid the waste. In this section, you will be challenged to answer three very important questions so that you can and WILL get to the root of the problem and rid the waste. You may write your answers out, or you can answer these questions aloud. Please see the example below. Please utilize examples in the following sections.

QUESTIONS TO PONDER

1. Does this situation, person or thing contribute to my overall mental well-being?
2. What am I losing if I decide no longer to engage in this behavior/activity?
3. What are 1-3 realistic questions to ponder when making decisions to move forward in life?

FEEL (INGS)

Hindrance: _____

Rid the waste: _____

COMMITMENT

Hindrance: _____

Rid the waste: _____

ABILITY

Hindrance: _____

Rid the waste: _____

EVOLUTION

Hindrance: _____

Rid the waste: _____

SELF-OBSERVATION

Describe how you displayed skills of the previous lesson.

_____

_____

_____

IMPACT

Describe how you have demonstrated impact in your life over the past 30 days.

_____

_____

_____

NURTURE

Describe how you have demonstrated nurture in your life over the past 30 days.

_____

_____

_____

PREPARATION

Describe how you have demonstrated preparation in your life over the past 30 days.

_____

_____

_____

Whether we choose to identify and/or recognize defaults, roadblocks, hurdles and U-turns in life, they will surface from time to time. Even in the midst of thriving and making progress, there will be inconveniences and life's circumstances that happen and sometimes set us back, BUT they allow us to learn from these situations and make better and different decisions while learning new ways to balance life. The key is holding ourselves accountable and learning to recognize what it is that's keeping us from becoming who and what we desire to be and learning how to rid the waste. In this section, you will be challenged to answer three very important questions so that you can and WILL get to the root of the problem and rid the waste. You may write your answers out, or you can answer these questions aloud. Please see the example below. Please utilize examples in the following sections.

QUESTIONS TO PONDER

1. Does this situation, person or thing contribute to my overall mental well-being?
2. What am I losing if I decide no longer to engage in this behavior/activity?
3. What are 1-3 realistic questions to ponder when making decisions to move forward in life?

IMPACT

Hindrance: _____

Rid the waste: _____

NURTURE

Hindrance: _____

Rid the waste: _____

PREPARATION

Hindrance: _____

Rid the waste: _____

SELF-OBSERVATION

Describe how you displayed skills of the previous lesson.

_____

_____

_____

TRANSFORMATION

Describe how you have demonstrated transformation in your life over the past 30 days.

_____

_____

_____

RESET

Describe how you have demonstrated a reset in your life over the past 30 days.

_____

_____

_____

TRANSITION

Describe how you have demonstrated transition in your life over the past 30 days.

_____

_____

_____

TRANSPARENCY

Describe how you have demonstrated transparency in your life over the past 30 days.

_____

_____

_____

Whether we choose to identify and/or recognize defaults, roadblocks, hurdles and U-turns in life, they will surface from time to time. Even in the midst of thriving and making progress, there will be inconveniences and life's circumstances that happen and sometimes set us back, BUT they allow us to learn from these situations and make better and different decisions while learning new ways to balance life. The key is holding ourselves accountable and learning to recognize what it is that's keeping us from becoming who and what we desire to be and learning how to rid the waste. In this section, you will be challenged to answer three very important questions so that you can and WILL get to the root of the problem and rid the waste. You may write your answers out, or you can answer these questions aloud. Please see the example below. Please utilize examples in the following sections.

QUESTIONS TO PONDER

1. Does this situation, person or thing contribute to my overall mental well-being?
2. What am I losing if I decide no longer to engage in this behavior/activity?
3. What are 1-3 realistic questions to ponder when making decisions to move forward in life?

TRANSFORMATION

Hindrance: _____

Rid the waste: _____

RESET

Hindrance: _____

Rid the waste: _____

TRANSITION

Hindrance: _____

Rid the waste: _____

TRANSPARENCY

Hindrance: _____

Rid the waste: _____

SELF-OBSERVATION

Describe how you displayed skills of the previous lesson.

_____

_____

_____

EXECUTION

Describe how you have demonstrated execution in your life over the past 30 days.

_____

_____

_____

VISION

Describe how you have demonstrated vision in your life over the past 30 days.

_____

_____

_____

PRODUCTIVITY

Describe how you have demonstrated productivity in your life over the past 30 days.

_____

_____

_____

Whether we choose to identify and/or recognize defaults, roadblocks, hurdles and U-turns in life, they will surface from time to time. Even in the midst of thriving and making progress, there will be inconveniences and life's circumstances that happen and sometimes set us back, BUT they allow us to learn from these situations and make better and different decisions while learning new ways to balance life. The key is holding ourselves accountable and learning to recognize what it is that's keeping us from becoming who and what we desire to be and learning how to rid the waste. In this section, you will be challenged to answer three very important questions so that you can and WILL get to the root of the problem and rid the waste. You may write your answers out, or you can answer these questions aloud. Please see the example below. Please utilize examples in the following sections.

QUESTIONS TO PONDER

1. Does this situation, person or thing contribute to my overall mental well-being?
2. What am I losing if I decide no longer to engage in this behavior/activity?
3. What are 1-3 realistic questions to ponder when making decisions to move forward in life?

EXECUTION

Hindrance: _____

Rid the waste: _____

VISION

Hindrance: _____

Rid the waste: _____

PRODUCTIVITY

Hindrance: _____

Rid the waste: _____

SELF-OBSERVATION

Describe how you displayed skills of the previous lesson.

_____

_____

_____

PURSUIT

Describe how you have demonstrated pursuit in your life over the past 30 days.

_____

_____

_____

STABILITY

Describe how you have demonstrated stability in your life over the past 30 days.

_____

_____

_____

INTRIGUE

Describe how you have demonstrated intrigue/intriguing abilities in your life over the past 30 days.

_____

_____

_____

Whether we choose to identify and/or recognize defaults, roadblocks, hurdles and U-turns in life, they will surface from time to time. Even in the midst of thriving and making progress, there will be inconveniences and life's circumstances that happen and sometimes set us back, BUT they allow us to learn from these situations and make better and different decisions while learning new ways to balance life. The key is holding ourselves accountable and learning to recognize what it is that's keeping us from becoming who and what we desire to be and learning how to rid the waste. In this section, you will be challenged to answer three very important questions so that you can and WILL get to the root of the problem and rid the waste. You may write your answers out, or you can answer these questions aloud. Please see the example below. Please utilize examples in the following sections.

QUESTIONS TO PONDER

1. Does this situation, person or thing contribute to my overall mental well-being?
2. What am I losing if I decide no longer to engage in this behavior/activity?
3. What are 1-3 realistic questions to ponder when making decisions to move forward in life?

PURSUIT

Hindrance: _____

Rid the waste: _____

STABILITY

Hindrance: _____

Rid the waste: _____

INTRIGUE/INTRIGUING

Hindrance: _____

Rid the waste: _____

SELF-OBSERVATION

Describe how you displayed skills of the previous lesson.

_____

_____

_____

ENVISION

Describe how you have demonstrated envision in your life over the past 30 days.

_____

_____

_____

DILIGENCE

Describe how you have demonstrated diligence in your life over the past 30 days.

_____

_____

_____

EMBODY

Describe how you have demonstrated embody/embodying in your life over the past 30 days.

_____

_____

_____

PATIENCE

Describe how you have demonstrated patience in your life over the past 30 days.

_____

_____

_____

Whether we choose to identify and/or recognize defaults, roadblocks, hurdles and U-turns in life, they will surface from time to time. Even in the midst of thriving and making progress, there will be inconveniences and life's circumstances that happen and sometimes set us back, BUT they allow us to learn from these situations and make better and different decisions while learning new ways to balance life. The key is holding ourselves accountable and learning to recognize what it is that's keeping us from becoming who and what we desire to be and learning how to rid the waste. In this section, you will be challenged to answer three very important questions so that you can and WILL get to the root of the problem and rid the waste. You may write your answers out, or you can answer these questions aloud. Please see the example below. Please utilize examples in the following sections.

QUESTIONS TO PONDER

1. Does this situation, person or thing contribute to my overall mental well-being?
2. What am I losing if I decide no longer to engage in this behavior/activity?
3. What are 1-3 realistic questions to ponder when making decisions to move forward in life?

ENVISION

Hindrance: _____

Rid the waste: _____

DILIGENCE

Hindrance: _____

Rid the waste: _____

EMBODY/EMBODYING

Hindrance: _____

Rid the waste: _____

PATIENCE

Hindrance: _____

Rid the waste: _____

SELF-OBSERVATION

Describe how you displayed skills of the previous lesson.

_____

_____

_____

ASSERTIVENESS

Describe how you have demonstrated assertiveness in your life over the past 30 days.

_____

_____

_____

TRANQUILITY

Describe how you have demonstrated tranquility in your life over the past 30 days.

_____

_____

_____

POSSIBILITY

Describe how you have demonstrated possibility in your life over the past 30 days.

_____

_____

_____

Whether we choose to identify and/or recognize defaults, roadblocks, hurdles and U-turns in life, they will surface from time to time. Even in the midst of thriving and making progress, there will be inconveniences and life's circumstances that happen and sometimes set us back, BUT they allow us to learn from these situations and make better and different decisions while learning new ways to balance life. The key is holding ourselves accountable and learning to recognize what it is that's keeping us from becoming who and what we desire to be and learning how to rid the waste. In this section, you will be challenged to answer three very important questions so that you can and WILL get to the root of the problem and rid the waste. You may write your answers out, or you can answer these questions aloud. Please see the example below. Please utilize examples in the following sections.

QUESTIONS TO PONDER

1. Does this situation, person or thing contribute to my overall mental well-being?
2. What am I losing if I decide no longer to engage in this behavior/activity?
3. What are 1-3 realistic questions to ponder when making decisions to move forward in life?

ASSERTIVENESS

Hindrance: _____

Rid the waste: _____

TRANQUILITY

Hindrance: _____

Rid the waste: _____

POSSIBILITY

Hindrance: _____

Rid the waste: _____

SELF-OBSERVATION

Describe how you displayed skills of the previous lesson.

_____

_____

_____

BRAVERY

Describe how you have demonstrated bravery in your life over the past 30 days.

_____

_____

_____

RECEPTIVE

Describe how you have demonstrated receptive/reception in your life over the past 30 days.

_____

_____

_____

MODEST

Describe how you have demonstrated modest/modesty in your life over the past 30 days.

_____

_____

_____

Whether we choose to identify and/or recognize defaults, roadblocks, hurdles and U-turns in life, they will surface from time to time. Even in the midst of thriving and making progress, there will be inconveniences and life's circumstances that happen and sometimes set us back, BUT they allow us to learn from these situations and make better and different decisions while learning new ways to balance life. The key is holding ourselves accountable and learning to recognize what it is that's keeping us from becoming who and what we desire to be and learning how to rid the waste. In this section, you will be challenged to answer three very important questions so that you can and WILL get to the root of the problem and rid the waste. You may write your answers out, or you can answer these questions aloud. Please see the example below. Please utilize examples in the following sections.

QUESTIONS TO PONDER

1. Does this situation, person or thing contribute to my overall mental well-being?
2. What am I losing if I decide no longer to engage in this behavior/activity?
3. What are 1-3 realistic questions to ponder when making decisions to move forward in life?

BRAVERY

Hindrance: _____

Rid the waste: _____

RECEPTIVE

Hindrance: _____

Rid the waste: _____

MODEST

Hindrance: _____

Rid the waste: _____

FREEDOM

Write here what freedom looks like for you and in your life. Listed below are different areas in which you can explore and describe what it means to you. Remember to be kind and gentle but *real* with yourself. Use this guide to identify, explore and make pertinent adjustments to your life.

SPIRITUAL LIFE

_____

_____

_____

Adjustments needed in my life to become freer in my spiritual life:

- _____

- _____

- _____

FINANCIAL LIFE

_____

_____

_____

Adjustments needed in my life to become freer in my financial life:

- _____

- _____

- _____

MENTAL LIFE

_____

_____

_____

Adjustments needed in my life to become freer in my mental life:

- _____
- _____
- _____

EMOTIONAL LIFE

_____

_____

_____

Adjustments needed in my life to become freer in my emotional life:

- _____
- _____
- _____

RELATIONSHIP LIFE

_____

_____

_____

Adjustments needed in my life to become freer in my relationship life:

- _____

- _____

- _____

www.ingramcontent.com/pod-product-compliance
Lightning Source LLC
Chambersburg PA
CBHW042353070526
44585CB00028B/2908